Practical Guide to Awareness
Discovering Your True Purpose

By Susan Nefzger

ISBN-13: 978-1983603396
ISBN-10: 1983603392

A Practical Guide to
Awareness

Susan Nefzger

Dedication:
Write the word of truth to those who hear.

Contents

Preface

Walking out into the ruins of Glastonbury Abbey, I traveled to a place that flowed within.

Inspired by surroundings of my distant past, I began to write. This was the beginning of what was to become my awakening and transformation.

Traveling on a personal vision quest my entire life, I have been on my way here— to this place.

My inner drive, restlessness and unspoken capacity define this moment in time.

Sitting amidst the floral abundance that lazily swings in the delicate breeze, light flickering under the leaves, I feel a wondrous gratitude. I travel in my mind's eye to the place and time of another existence...of a memory. The touch of the stone brings it all back. The vibration of old continues... it never dies. The Abbey, this place… remains a haven for all that is holy and good.

Creation is abundant here, growing, changing, dreaming simultaneously. The earth grows, the seasons change and we dream of moments such as this in the garden of solitude among the buzzing bees pollinating the flowers.

I close my eyes and drift into dreaming...

The stone arches are witnesses to history of many types, events we know and others forever secret, except in the vibrations of the stone. Yes, bloody endings occurred here in physical form. All who came to this peaceful sanctuary have felt the magnetic pull. But each had a purpose and fulfilled it, some knowing they would be forever altered by the very act of completing their vision quest.

Susan Nefzger

Glastonbury Abbey, Somerset, UK

May 2015

Introduction

Upon arrival from London, we were initiated in a beautiful opening ceremony to begin the Conscious Writing retreat at The Abbey House in Glastonbury, Somerset, UK in May of 2015.

As the opening ceremony of the retreat concluded, I was dying to walk out into the Glastonbury Abbey ruins, but the gate was locked as the sun was setting. Promenading in the lush gardens of Abbey House, a Raven as large as a lap dog, dark as the darkest night, greeted me with his raucous hello. So, I answered him, in disbelief actually—marveling at his size which seemed bigger than a normal raven. He walked away from me then, staking his territory, having made his presence known.

Thank you, sentry of old, the Raven.

Each day since that first evening introduction, he greets me in the early morn beneath my window, cawing loudly, rah rah rah! He urges me with a wakeup call that cannot be ignored. I wake from half sleep, hearing also the morning sounds so sweet, twittering birds chirping, church bells ringing in a new day that is cold and cloudy. But like a flower, the day will open and change before my eyes, brightening, glistening and awakening with the sunrise.

The Raven has come to wake me... singing his loud signal —caw caw caw... a wakeup call!

Yes, a wakeup call. That is the reason I am here; to bring my gift to the world by writing this book.

The words that appear here have been channeled from Source and are meant to inspire and uplift. At the same time the words are clear information about finding out who you truly are at the soul level in order to be happy and alive with passion to share your gift with the world.

The chapters are a juxtaposition of the practical guide and a tale of a woman's journey of faith with her true love. Her steadfast adherence to a divinely inspired path despite obstacles such as geographical journeys, death, public criticism, and threat of religious persecution is an inspiration. She has led me through my darkest days in the last 2 years and provided me with the vision to do so—with as much grace as possible. To her, I take my hat off in gratitude.

1.
Personal Awareness

Personal awareness begins at the soul level, and is the perception of oneself at the soul level. So, what is self-perception? Ask yourself this question- what is the soul of my being?

It is the purest essence of your spirit not your body or mind.

Try to sit in a quiet place and see your dreams. See your perfect world. In your mind or on paper, put together an album of pictures that depicts an ideal world for you. *These images are you. They represent how you see yourself. Try to inject as much freedom and peace as possible to develop the vision. Do you feel free and at peace?*

Now, hear the wind blowing, the leaves crackling, the bees buzzing, the birds singing, the water rippling and the waves crashing. Try and perceive your surroundings with your whole self. Then ask yourself, what is perception?

These questions may assist you:

- What is your perception of who you are?

- Are you aware of who you are at the soul level?

- How does your self-perception compare to how others see you?

- And finally—do the two paint the same picture? Because if they don't there may be

- a disconnect between how you show yourself to the world and who you truly are.

Giving yourself permission to answer these questions truthfully will provide a jumping off point toward heightened self-awareness. This is the first step toward achieving an unvarnished view of who you are at the soul level.

After you have an album of images, see how much better you feel by changing the images to suit your inner happiness or peace. See how specific changes to the album reflect your feelings.

It can be eye opening. Just try it. Later, reflect on this inner discourse. Then journal it if you feel inclined, it can help you later on as we delve deeper into self-awareness.

11.
Personal Awareness and the Collective Consciousness

Some of you may be asking what is the Collective Consciousness?

The answer is simple, it is the group thought and consciousness that you are involved in at the soul level. The difference between self-perception and the Collective Consciousness and why it matters is that you all contribute to the energy of this group. They may include your family, friends and other people you interact with on a daily basis and have known for years. The energy interacts with all other soul groups to form a collective that continually moves us as individuals to the level of enlightenment necessary to evolve as human beings. That is the goal.

Each soul is unique and has a gift to share with the world— including you.

Self-perception matters to the Collective Consciousness because if you are unaware of who you are at the soul level and what gift you possess, then you probably are not doing your part to elevate the consciousness of your soul group and by definition, the world. <u>Not yet, anyway.</u>

The reason we exist is to share our gift throughout the world we inhabit.

The Collective Consciousness is the energetic creator which forms the fabric of humanity and we are each a thread, co-creating the fabric as we weave and are woven together. Each connected and connecting, to add strength to each other and enhance our vibration. Just like a sock or a shirt, the fabric of humanity contains weaknesses that may need mending at times. Such as when daily life brings us down, we as humans become weary and need support.

The key to breathing life into the fabric of humanity is to recognize that we are all one.

Without the other we cannot exist... but together we strengthen each other. We do so through our shared wisdom, strengths, weaknesses and inspirations.

We aspire to bring the best intentions into the world- to try to help others in creating a peaceful world. Love is the ultimate purpose for each of us, because without love we will not discover ourselves.

This brings us Dear Reader, to the point in our exercise where we *consciously choose.*

Every choice contains consequences. WE make the choice to be afraid or not to be. WE make the choice to feel love or fear. So many times, as humans we REACT. Reaction based on history, beliefs or negative experiences can sometimes shape our present moment. Yet, it is based on the past.

We can only be in the moment we are in right now. That is all that exists. Remembering this by being present and not on auto pilot is a life changer, because then you allow yourself to consciously align and be open to all possibilities.

Figuring out who you are and what makes you happy is number one to discovering your true purpose.

In doing so, you will learn to do that which fulfills you and you will be present in that joy.

It is important to consciously choose so that your external circumstances do not determine your reality. But your inner joy will create a day filled with positivity and hopefulness so that the external −no matter what it happens to be—is manageable.

As this journey of faith begins, we share a tale of reminiscence as a holy woman recalls her life's path, propelled by the promise of a new world where love is the key to all life. Knowing unconditional love by her birthright and through her lifelong faith community she fulfills her commitment through doubts, trials, tribulation, death, and an unspoken bond with one who has gone before her.

111.
The Bond

As the light fades on a tumultuous day, I reflect on the Creator's plan; love, forgiveness, healing and everlasting life are the hallmarks of the way forward.

In spirit, we dance together in the light. For we are all one. Our soul mates sparkling and twinkling with recognition at last! We embody the feelings of deepest gratitude and love toward one another. Can we go out into the physical world and continue the quest, we ask ourselves?

Even our spirit wonders as we drift apart to join our bodies in the physical world.

Yes, we can stay on the path with renewed purpose, for our purpose as light workers binds us together, inalterably linked. We call on our bond as light workers reunited to move forward on the road ahead. Doubts as well as our unbounded happiness at being together, fill our conscious hearts. It is an unusual feeling to be sure. But our renewal has a purpose and we move into that light space, into the unconditional love vibration, in order to begin and end our days with hope for the manifestation of our dreams.

The purpose of our lives is to share our gift, our own individual gift, with the world in order to help others. Why are we here if not to help others experience a fruitful and positive life?

Recalling the memory of a vow I made to my love, "my life, my love, my divinely guided plan that all must one day be made aware. Are we to perish without the knowing? Without the love?

There is no equal love known to man or woman. Only in spirit and alignment can one know the true word."

IV.
The Purpose of Commitment in Relationships

C ommitment is a word that is often used and possibly little understood. For that reason, let's explore the purpose of commitment as it relates to awareness in relationships, in our spiritual lives and in relationship to our self-care.

We can choose to make a commitment to tenets which create a life of awareness, as mentioned above, within our relationships, in our spiritual lives and especially in caring for ourselves in order to be available on a positive level for our loved ones, family and friends. Being aware brings presence.

We can practice committing to awareness in all of these aspects. Here, our discussion begins with relationships.

What is the purpose of commitment in a relationship?

A decision to bring ourselves wholly and completely into a relationship with a child, a sibling, a parent, a friend or a lover is a commitment. Because, as that bond is created, many facets of energetic exchange occur. For example, committing to being loving, open and respectful is conducive to one's well-being. Being present allows us to focus on the practice of maintaining awareness. With the act of being aware we can honor our commitment to ourselves and our loved ones by being present. In doing so we remain honest with ourselves and our loved ones because we are in the moment —aware of what we are committing to. If we walk around on auto-pilot and do things the same way every day, without being aware of where we go and what we do, and how we do it, we are not present. That sometimes allows for events to happen that take us beyond what we are capable of handling with ease and grace. This can lead to problems in inter-personal relationships that have the potential to cause break- ups, arguments, unrealistic expectations, and so on.

It may help to create a space in your daily life that brings you to awareness, whether by affir-mation, meditation or a practice recognizing the commitments in your life. In that way we review our responsibility to ourselves and others with calmness and patience before we are confronted with an issue. We can then allow ourselves to handle any issues that arise.

$\mathcal{V}.$
The Vow

In the present moment I stand before you, heart to heart and soul to soul. What lies ahead for us, we cannot know. The wind of winter brings with it a longing for days past, running in the green meadows, climbing in the dusty hills and loving under the stars.

We contemplate the fire before us as we vow to belong to one another forever. We are warmed in the knowledge of our deep love and commitment.

How long do we have together? We wonder... as we clasp hands and join lips in embrace.

Vast openness in front of us, we view the galaxy and we ride the star scapes to the heavens.

Love --and all that it entails —is awaiting us in the embodiment of who we are together. We smile with the knowing that our soul connection takes us to worlds near and far. Through separation, fear, death and new life we will find each other, whatever happens. We will know each other, no matter the physical appearance.

What of our soul group? Will we remain intact? We ponder this as the fire crackles and spits, the kindling catches the spark and lights brilliantly — giving life to the flame. We are comforted by the bright warm flame, the flame of a fiery soul bringing forth its light for all to see. That is our mission-- to help all become aware so their light may shine.

Settling into night the dogs asleep by the fire, night wind howling, horses now calm and sleepy, we gaze upward into the heavens. In our knowing a certainty exists-- that whether we live another day, we will meet again, as we revel in the love that surrounds us, through nature's bounty and its harshness. We have a strong faith. The faith the of the Ancients – as foretold by our elders and passed down through time. We feel the collective energy of the Universe and know we are protected in our love for each other.

Wrapping ourselves up against the cold night, we lie in warmth. Warmth of love, of light, of faith. A mission is ours to keep and hold. We will fulfill it for those who come after us. We will know success as we sleep, we send blessings to those who carry the torch of Universal truth to the future world. Gratefully hold the space of love and peace to that ideal- in hopes that the faith we hold passes on in the souls of our dear ones. Sleepy, falling down into dreaming, we go together traveling once again to our homeland... aware that we cannot go there in body. But happy now, we go in spirit.

$\mathcal{VI}.$
Commitment to Spirituality and Self Care

Committing to spirituality is part of our awareness-seeking path because without spirituality we cannot feel connected to ourselves, let alone the greater good. How you ask does spirituality help us feel connected to our true selves? First you must understand what your spirituality is to you.

What is your spirituality?

It can vary from person to person but most importantly what is it to you?

When you answer the question; honor that and what it means as your definition of spirituality.

Being, loving, seeing the energy that surrounds us and believing in the goodness of all and of the Creator or Source— that is spiritual awareness to me. Seeing life on the Universal scale— how all events are connected, not just as limited to the microcosm of one's daily life, helps us understand how the fabric of life enjoins all of us.

The key is to trust your inner guide to show you the correct path for you. In all areas, listen to that inner voice, even with seemingly inconsequential decisions – especially if you hear direction.

Try it and make a note of how things turn out. Then track how your life changes over a week, a month, several months and a year. You will begin to observe the difference and your subconscious will get used to listening to itself for direction.

Respecting everyone on the journey toward awareness and spirituality is important. It helps keep the threads of interconnection woven and strongly bound in the fabric of humanity.

This leads us to the subject of self-care, Dear Ones. For how can we support the fabric of humanity with our contributions if we ourselves are not well, happy and purposeful because we are not utilizing our gifts?

In seeking this level of awareness, we inspire others to do so. You may be asking yourself, *how can I inspire anyone else?* One can inspire in many ways. But putting other's before yourself whittles away the soul. So, take care not to do so because you may be left with no reserves. Without a passion or a soul purpose we do not have the energy to help, much less inspire others.

Making self-care a priority leads to enhanced energy, greater happiness and the ability to manage all the activities and commitments in our lives. Maintaining your physical health, spiritual health and emotional health contributes to a unified, balanced spirit. It is the most important tenet of awareness.

Sometimes without self-care, comes illness of varying forms. Mental illness, physical illness, accidents, etc... you have a choice. Mind-body awareness alerts you to anything going on that may begin to build disease in your physical form. It keeps you on the path of wellness and mindfulness to be aware of your health and what is going on in your body.

EXERCISE IN MINDFULNESS

Take a few minutes each day to sit in silence. Clear your mind... take as long as you need.

However long it takes until your mind is not worrying about your daily work, the kids, the dog, your partner. Now when you are empty minded just sit in that peaceful stillness —that IS you at the soul level. Stay in that space as long as you can. Increase the time each day. It will actually improve your health and well-being by connecting you to your soul.

By connecting with your soul, you are connecting to Source. We are part of Source or God, whatever name you give the Creator. We are not separate we are a unit of God. Mindfulness at the soul level brings us back to Source and oneness. Thus, avoiding misalignment and eventual unhappiness and disease.

VII.
Secret Destination

Night into day, we make our way through the terraced hills of green. Though it has been but days, it feels like years away from our homeland. Onward trekking, we travel the highway of faith. We carry a burden, yet also the harbinger of a new way for those who believe. This is such a different place, here in Glastonbury, lush and wet and cold. Unlike the desert, our home, dry and hot. This land is alive!

The magic springs with the water that heals, essential to the mission as we carry the Cup to keep in our family. Will we fulfill our destiny to the One who left us in body? Our hearts are full as we ride on toward our destination, to live a life undetected and anonymous in this beautiful place. A land so quiet yet musical with the birdsong like a concert surrounding us.

Journeymen, we go on a metaphysical path, yet physical in its origins. From birthplace to deathbed, it is apparent we may never witness again what we had in our homeland.

As the tale unfolds, it occurs to me Dear Reader that you would like to know its origins.

I may well confide in you with tears in my eyes and pain in my heart, as I walk through the memory. The persecution of truth leading up to the death of our leader, as his blood dripping on the hot sand, I hear the overwhelming sounds of buzzing, as thousands of flies surround and land on the crucified bodies hanging. Looking up, I see him on the deathbed they made for him, mangled and bleeding from every part of his battered body. The pain he feels I feel in my heart, as it is crushed with sorrow. Stifling hot, I cannot breathe; I am suffocating from sorrow. Those of us who were present know the truth of that day as it is forever emblazoned on our souls. We are torn in emotions from body and mind and soul. We feel the depth of the moment as it surrounds us, while our followers cower in fear and stumble from the weight of the loss, our collective loss. The skies darken and his soul leaves the planet... as we go into hiding, yet to be in the world as truth bearers.

We must travel away or be killed before we honor our agreement to continue the movement of love and peace.

The day was hot and dusty like any other only it wasn't like any other day. Tired and thirsty we stopped to rest after traveling through the night from home. It would be a long journey across the sea. Now on horseback we feel the burden of the knowledge we carried.

$\mathcal{V}III.$
The Journey

How and why is it important to be present *on the journey toward awareness?*

Thus far, we've explored self-perception at the soul level, and how that relates to the Collective Consciousness, to commitment and how we can apply this inner knowledge to our daily lives. We now understand Dear Reader, that if we are unaware of opportunities along the path to awareness we may take longer to arrive at our purposeful destination.

If you are reading this you ARE questing.

You are searching for the essence to complete your soul, to fill a hole inside that you may not be able to identify. Some people experience a constant restlessness, while others turn to drugs, alcohol, or even work to find happiness or to anesthetize the feeling that something is missing in their lives.

People are often not aware that there are a wide variety of spiritual practices which enable us to live in this world and feel better! All too often we try a particular method of achieving awareness because it worked for a friend or a family member. However, each individual has a separate path— a sometimes lonely road. So, if one method does not work try another until you find a comfort level. Some evolve quickly while for others it takes lifetimes of living and learning. This is as it should be —given each human's experience, because we all have a choice.

If you feel something is missing in your life and wish to hear a drumbeat that is meant for you alone, then start applying these practices. If you can cultivate awareness through the steps outlined here, the answer will be revealed to you Dear Reader.

We must wake up to awareness. One cannot see the breadcrumbs on the path with eyes closed. Opportunities for awareness present themselves in many forms. But please know that there are no missed opportunities! The Universe has a plan for you so the simplest way is to remain open to all opportunities.

Being open means committing to embracing each day not by what is scheduled, or what you think you should be doing, but by staying alert to anything that makes you happy, excited and grateful.

That doesn't mean going shopping and buying new things. Rather, we are talking about happiness at the innermost core of your being. Not what your intellect tells you … but what your heart is telling you.

For example, if your work leaves you disillusioned, stressed out and unhappy, chances are it's not fulfilling your soul purpose. Nature is often a source of inspiration, as is music, art and helping animals or other people who are in need. Whatever leaves you feeling positive and contributing to something greater than yourself, that is the beginning of knowing. Explore that avenue; see where it takes you.

Be open to change! The conversation I like to have with fellow travelers is one of trusting.

People are so ruled by their fears that they don't trust in a higher order. You can always come up with a reason NOT to do something, especially if it's different or takes you out of your comfort zone. Fear often focuses on disaster such as losing status, money or acceptance. To avoid such losses, some people live a whole lifetime doing what they think they should. This can lead to illness and feeling unfulfilled. *Could any material loss be worse than the ever-searching emptiness of living a life unfulfilled?*

The alternative to fear is love and trust. Focus on what you want and move forward with love.

Taking the chance to create a meaningful life by believing in yourself, will lead to happiness. You can always make a list of "what-ifs", but you won't avoid them by writing them down. Believe and trust that being in the present moment leads to synchronicity which opens up the availability for opportunity.

Your journey may have twists and turns and that is ok. Arriving at the destination may not be an obvious or straightforward road.

Remember the fabric of life? Your life is the same, it is a thread interwoven with the endless other threads that make up your world fabric. Each thread contributes to the strength of the whole. When you feel fearful and need comfort, wrap the fabric around you like a blanket. Try to use this feeling of comfort to give you courage on your path, so you can discover your true gift.

IX.
Remembrance

I feel a twinge of melancholy and trepidation, as I gaze at the sparkling light on the jet-black sea we have just crossed. A sense of foreboding overcomes me. *"Do not fear"*, I say to myself as I send a heartfelt prayer to the heavens. The answer to my prayer reveals itself in my heart: "All will be well as you trust in the power of those who guide you. As above, so below. We are with you as we have always been throughout time immemorial. You are blessed with a faithful heart. All the world will benefit from your actions for centuries to come. Do not fear, Dear One."

With this message I am strengthened and can breathe deeply in my faith. A calm overcomes me, enveloped by a sense of belonging to a larger purpose.

In the knowing comes the realization that

we have chosen and prepared for this from the beginning of time. Each on a path to share our gift with the world. What is my gift then? To be the keeper of the word? To have carried the Holy Cup to its final resting place? I return to the present moment by the signal from my fellow travelers, that we must hasten our journey.

We are on a path to the meeting place. It is one of divine origin as told. As the rain seeps into our cloaks in the richness of the landscape of Glastonbury, I question myself, *to what end this?*

In all of my life I've not felt the doubts I have had since we left our home. I try to leave the doubts behind and trust in my path with the divine right that accompanies it. To no avail. The deep mysteries of the new land leave me in question. Magic surrounds us but I feel uncertain.

Committed, we go to the appointed place through the cold, wet night. Yet, we dwell on our past, feeling warm in our hearts. Those halcyon days seem so long ago! The days of old were a peaceful sharing of the message of love. Emboldened by the truth, the certainty in our hearts helped us stay true in maintaining the word. Trusting, knowing, feeling the path of the word as One Truth, we had all we needed in our commune by the sea. How I miss it so!

I close my eyes and dream... as I smell the

salty air, hear the seabirds cry and the gentle waves lapping on the shore.

As the Moon waxes we approach our destination, a friendly place to shelter, glad for the warmth of a fire inside the stone walls of a blessed place. An ally to bring into our circle in this new world. As we now stop for the night— bone weary, cold and with much trepidation, we enter the space. Have we done the right thing to follow this mission? At once we feel the love, the divine energy that led us here. It fills us and we know beyond a doubt that yes, our mission is at an end for now. We can rest in peace.

𝒳.
Commitment to Awareness

Commit to awareness so you can share your gift with others.

When we are interrupted by the daily, mundane tasks of life, we must try to integrate them with patience. Spiritual practice is a commitment, like any other important part of our lives. Commit to spirituality just as you commit to daily exercise, your work, and your family activities. *Spirituality is critical to awareness because it is that deep inner peace of knowing that all is provided, all is inspired and all is for a higher purpose.*

Awakening to what you may ask? When one is spiritually aware the pressures of life are less so by being able to see the big picture at work. With a different perspective such as this, the material world no longer holds so much power over our thoughts and actions.

Now, staying awake is the difficult part. This is why a commitment is essential. To reap the rewards of awareness, one must try to live with mind and heart in a spiritual environment. So now you ask, what is a spiritual environment?

Here are a few ideas to help you understand.

1. Honoring people, animals and places for who they are as they are.

2. Trying to accept, instead of change people.

3. Being non-judgmental with those who are different. Trying not to judge other's lives or decisions, is the key to awareness. Your beliefs may be different and that is fine.

4. Even if people are mean or hurtful toward you let it go. It matters not for each of us has a path to follow. Bless them and be grateful you are not in a place of darkness or sadness such as they.

5. Showing love to all people is essential to maintaining a spiritual practice.

6. Being joyful! Joy is contagious. Give thanks each day for your blessings. Bring joy to others with a smile.

7. Helping others if you can do so. Help your family, your friends, your neighbors and others with your soul capacity. Don't hide your light, let it shine!

8. Sharing your light with others who need it most. Sometimes we come in contact with people or situations that allow us to feel uncomfortable. In these instances, try to determine why you feel that way, without attachment. You can dispel whatever is bothering you about the situation or person if you are not attached. Stay on the path in the energy of helpfulness.

XI.
Death and Loss

We pause and with heavy hearts we faithfully remember our leader who represented the Christ Consciousness of unconditional love. This is a part of our history in the larger world apart from the value it holds for our family.

Heartbreak at the death of a loved one is difficult to describe. A permanent hole exists in my soul even though I understand the transition of spirit from the body upon death.

I know they are here with us and everywhere in the ether, yet the physical loss is numbing. The earth connection of our body and another's spirit never dies...

In this foreign land, we complete our first meal with the Cup that was used for delivering the message of love at the final meeting of our word bearers, our disciples. I feel a second wave of grief and heartbreaking loss. Why, I want to yell to the world!

But for now, the movement must carry on so that he did not die in vain. <u>We must carry the truth not the dogma to the world as we've been told by the "church."</u> The truth is that our savior did not come to transform people in judgement, he came to deliver the word that love is all there is.... unconditional love. That is it. The world cannot remain as it is.

We silently mourn in this eternal place meant for legends. Memories filter through me... in my mind's eye I see the images of our life together. Playing with him as a child, laughing tumbling, hiding in the trees. Playing as if we had forever together. And in that moment, we did have forever. For that moment lives on in my heart.

Now, we accept our destiny as we leave to spread the word. We will survive, not as we were, but as new people created by this experience of loss in our lives.

Keep a small place in your heart for the person you used to be. Never let it die. For without that piece of the puzzle your evolution is for naught. It is the constant reminder of your humanity. We all suffer and we all have doubts. Keep it, treasure it and love it. Do not hide it.

So onward we go, we walk the path in our minds and in our hearts as we start a new day.

The history lives on through us. No matter the trial or tribulation, we are guided by the One Love.

The love is the connection we share. Dear Ones, as we are each a thread in the great fabric of life, we keep weaving it through the bumps and snags. But we are always weaving the thread as part of the whole.

Never forget, never forget! And with the memory, keep the faith. The knowledge that we are provided for always.

Within each of us is the key. The choice is yours alone. The key unlocks the door to vast treasures that lie inside each of us.

$XII.$
Self-Care

Although it is not the first one mentioned here, self-care is the most important tenet by far.

Why you ask? Because without your health and well-being, you will have nothing to give to the world. For this reason, self-care (committing to take care of your own body and soul above the needs of others) precedes all the other tenets on the path to self-awareness.

If you don't even know how to *self-care* how will you be aware?

I can hear the responses now, Dear Reader. You say but I have children, a husband or partner, a job, a faith community, a charity. Yes, but it's true that if you are not happy, well and healthy, you cannot fulfill your commitments to those you love and cherish.

Let us discuss self-care in depth in order to help you understand from a self-perceptive point of view.

What do we mean by that phrase— self-care?

Putting our self first means taking care of what your soul thirsts for, before taking care of another's needs. Daily, weekly, monthly, whatever feels right to you. It is possible to take care of yourself and your needs along with other responsibilities.

For example, you feel better, more grounded and focused if you practice yoga each day.

Make the time to do so. You need not neglect your other commitments. But like being thirsty for water, you are thirsty deep in your soul for the answer to your questions and needs. Become more aware of how you serve, through the essence of your gift. Ask yourself the question, how do I serve humanity, my family, or my faith community?

Women often put themselves last in the scheme of family and work. They put everyone else's needs above their own. I really learned this in the past year while readying to move to a different geographic location without my son, who is now attending college. All of a sudden, I snapped, thinking why can't I live where I want when I want and where I am fulfilled and happy? Everyone can certainly take care of themselves, right? It hit me like a ton of bricks! Yes, I am living these words and acting these words now, and let me tell you something, it was not easy. A mother naturally puts her children's needs above her own.

We think we will be met with a negative response if we put ourselves first, and we have been conditioned to do so. But you must stand in your power.

Try to do one thing for yourself daily that lights your inner flame. Whatever that may be — like helping others you are drawn to in volunteer work, or take artistic or writing classes, learn a new language or activity! When you put your needs first it has a positive effect on those in your life, because you serve as an example, you are most likely happier, and definitely feel better about yourself than if you did not. Of course, consider how this decision will affect those in your life. Committing to self-care will help your children become more self-aware, independent and compassionate. They may even better understand other's needs through understanding your needs.

This leads to a more efficient self-care system for body and soul, which leads to a higher level of awareness.

Then as you are more aware, you understand the energy that surrounds us and how pertinent it is to the work we do. Your burden will be eased when you understand that all is not directed at you as a criticism, when things don't go your way.

Accepting others as they are, not as you wish them to be, even when they are negative, is key.

Detach your personal feelings from the negativity. Non-judgement is helpful because you can only be responsible for yourself, for how you choose to live. Fighting a battle that is not yours to fight can only lead to disillusionment.

Once we abandon the need to make all activity and interactions about us, we start to gain objective insight about others. Then we can discern how to best serve ourselves first in order to become self-aware. At that point you can serve others well and in times of need.

$XIII.$
Attachment and Letting Go

How do we allow for attachment to rule our lives? Is there an outcome or event that you hold on to or push for? Do you insist on the necessity of something in your life, which may cause a violation of the tenets mentioned in previous chapters? If so, that is attachment.

When you are so attached to the outcome of an action unable to envision any other conclusion— it changes your perception of the situation.

Impartial perception and objectivity are helpful in living a spiritual life. You may need to slowly disengage from your attachment in order to detach completely. For example, attachment to the distractions we choose can add stress to our daily lives. Such as overdoing exercise, work, alcohol, drugs, shopping or activities are all distractions from being present and self-aware. First consider why we are stressed out to begin with, is it from work or our kids? Only you know the answer to that question and it is an individual thing.

Be aware Dear Reader, when we do not trust that all will be provided for we drive ourselves to accomplish and we try to manage the outcome of activity to suit our purposes. When we do not believe in our own divinity, we end up doing harm to our bodies to relieve the stress. Maybe we are not going within to resolve these self-inflicted stressors or issues.

When stress strikes and we feel the urge to engage in harmful behavior, instead take a moment and breathe deeply, go outside and look at the sky. Change your perspective in order to healthfully manage the stress. In that regard, mindfulness is playing a role in allowing you to be present. The key to letting go of attachments is mindfulness. Experience all that is happening in the moment. The birds are tweeting, the wind is blowing, the sun is shining, and other details, such as this. Opportunities abound which open our hearts to endless possibilities. At this point, we are not on auto pilot. We are allowing for synchronicity to occur. We are alert to the possibilities.

Being Alert
Exercises:

1. Take a walk- whether in nature or in the city. Do you notice where and what it is that surrounds you? Try to say silently to yourself, "I'm walking on the sidewalk, I see blue sky, green palm fronds, and the blue-green ocean." In other words, describe the present moment to yourself. This allows for focus on the actions in order to remain present.

2. At work- being focused is often not difficult because you are there to do a job. But while you are focusing on your work, do so with a helpful nature. This positive attitude helps to lighten the energy and the mood, which lifts the atmosphere.

3. At home- we all understand how difficult it is to be present in our home life. Especially when dealing with our children, partners or parents. Staying present changes the dynamic drastically.

You will have more patience and experience a deeper connection with others, then everyone feels supported. Try to leave work and money issues as well as other problems aside when relating to your loved ones. Take one step at a time toward being present and you'll feel the difference in a positive way.

In today's world of information overload, the easiest way to be present is to leave technology out of the equation. Being aware of your surroundings without allowing numerous thoughts to distract your attention. Once you get accustomed to being present you will cultivate mindfulness which generates synchronicity. How? Again, by being aware and in the moment, you allow for the synchronicities to occur. They present themselves and you recognize and capitalize on what the Universe is offering you. Then you can accomplish tasks in a much simpler way and connect with all forms of being in the flow of energy surrounding you.

$\mathcal{XIV}$.
Truth and Choice

"As we go, so we are." I now realize that this mantra begins each day for me. With those words we move forward in faith and hope for a bright new day. At least we can *feel* that intention on our journey, no matter how the days begin or end. Now it is clear we have begun again.

The path is not always known to us, Dear Reader.

We must trust with a brave heart and if we doubt, so be it, but always know the plan begins with a choice. The choice is yours. Choose your intention for the day; believe all is possible and imbue your day with a clear purpose.

Try Dear Ones, to perceive the light of each day no matter the circumstance.

It is within you inside your heart. We all radiate

the light from our hearts. Follow your heart for that is the way of truth, through love.

Then, act each day from truth as you see how happy you are, but do so with a kind heart. Kindness helps ease the pain of certain realities. Sometimes others need to discover the truth in their time. For we are bearers of truth and as such we walk a special path. A path of darkness where we shed light and often one filled with days where we question it. Questioning is perfectly natural. Yet, we come back to the core truth of who we are and why we are here now.

Which leads us back to the beginning. The circle of life provides that all people are born with a unique gift. In order to discover, to learn, to know your gift, awareness is essential.

$\mathcal{XV}$.
Our Purpose

Why are we attempting to realize our true purpose?
Your purpose is written on your soul like a birthmark. It is clear if your eyes are open to see it.

As children, we are open to seeing all things. But as adults, we avoid facing hardship and negative issues. If we try to see the world as a child, without bias, we will experience it anew.

It may just change your day. Try it first for an hour or a few hours.

Then try the perspective change for longer durations and see how it affects how you live.

Finally try it for an entire day, do you feel different?

What do you observe? Can you recognize anything different in the way you perceive life? *Is it possible to hear the song your soul sings?* Even in the darkness it is singing to you. It is leading you if you can listen. For all is not as it appears and the perception of what is dark and what is light is not always the same to everyone.

I shall want to hear your answer Dear Reader.

Let us find beauty in our daily lives, wherever we are. One tiny detail of beauty. It is certainly within and around us. If you see someone in need of beauty, give it to them if you can. Walking down the street, I often pick flowers. Sometimes when I pass others I offer them a flower. It costs nothing and I have shared beauty with another person.

This, Dear Reader is the question. The answer is most telling. How do you help others?

If you remember, we asked ourselves this question when we began our light filled journey here together. You each have a gift to share with the world. Some share by building empires, some by building charities, and others give freely of their money to help others. Even the downtrodden have a gift to share. Those who feel compelled to lift up those who are sad, know that it need not cost anything to do so.

$XVI.$
Onward to Destiny

As I say morning prayers, the cool air drifts through the cloister[SW1] window, lightly caressing my cheek as I feel and smell the Spring, peaceful, silent and full of possibility. I finally gaze toward the meadows, green and alive with new growth. I am called to wander out to see the sun as it rises. Filled with gratitude for this beauty that surrounds me, I know the time has come to leave this place. I will leave a piece of myself here, my vibration.

As peace filled as our world is now, we must travel onward. I walk through the old trees, gazing at their branches and wondering what they have witnessed in their time here. Feeling the presence of their worldly wisdom, I am comforted. How I will miss this sacred ground I walk upon. I breathe deeply... thanking God for the sanctuary we have been given here in Glastonbury.

Leaving a part of ourselves here we can ensure that those who are on the path will discover the signs, and understand with love. We soon embark on our mission of bringing the word to those who seek it, in faith and community. It is our path and we may go our separate ways, depending on our calling. As we are called, we shall go. That was the pact we made as disciples of the One Love. To carry the word to all who will quest. We do so willingly and with strength and faith. We make ready for the journey to deliver the rest of the story and connect to the world.

We were forced to leave the homeland for this wondrous place which has given us a blessed refuge— calm, peaceful and abundant. In friendship, we created a holy place where the land had held the space for us. We do seek our destiny to keep alive our purpose and help others understand the story.

$XVII.$
New Life

A new life begins once we shed the old life. You may be wondering what that means. Dear Reader, within each of us lies a gift, a treasure that was buried when your soul transcended into the tiny creature you were born into. Musings, daydreams and feelings guide us as children on a path toward our passion. When you were a child, you probably said to yourself, "I want to be _____ when I grow up." This is your true self-perception and as adults we lose that sense of listening to our passionate heart. That is where your treasure is buried, within your heart and soul.

Some fortunate souls do hold on to their gift, which is embedded in their personality, as they grow and build their lives. They find a soul mate compatible with that journey. They move on to birthing their own children who will also receive a gift. Most people however, do not remember or choose to forget. Then later in life it hits them—they ask themselves, "what am I doing with my life?"

The fight goes on, for it will never die. The fight to keep and bring love to the world, to your life and family. Why must we engage in battle to deliver a gift you ask? It is a symbol for us – a reminder of what was sacrificed by those who have gone ahead of us. We must strive for a sense of conviction and purpose. For otherwise, we do not place a priority on the goals of such. That is the fight.

It is within each of us. Seeking, finding and staying true to the path that has been designated for you. It's easier to go along with the crowd. It is not easy at times to bring light to the darkest corners of the world. But we do so in order to share love. If you act from love, you will feel love and empathy. The more you clearly intend to do so, the more you will succeed in portraying the divine, which will serve as a role model for others. The more people you touch, the more will follow and that Dear Ones is meant as *the work*.

Go in love each day to be the shining example. Even when you are met with a wall of stone, turn and move on. For one day there may be a small opening in the wall through which you may enter with love. The road is paved with pitfalls. But if your intention is filled with love, you will find your way around danger.

Begin by serving as the light for those in the dark who cannot yet see the candle burning bright. Help others when they seek it from you. Try to keep the tenets in mind, as we have discussed. Remember the purpose of commitment to your relationships, to your spirituality and to your self-care. Not least important is your relationship to the Collective Consciousness.

You are now ready. This is the time when these words along with your understanding of them, demonstrate your path ahead.

Exercise in Meditation

Close your eyes and breathe deeply. Clear your mind and hear your heart song. Listen to its beat. That is your connection to the consciousness that surrounds you daily. As you breathe, let the breath fill your entire body. The essence of who you are is there, waiting for you to feel it. Once you have a clear mind, sit in silence as long as possible. Center yourself. Focus on the breath going in and out. Sit in clear minded silence as long as you can. Its ok if thoughts drift in, just watch them go out. Feel the center of your being now and stay in that feeling as long as you can. In the present, you are allowing for synchronicity. When you come out of meditation notice how calm and peaceful you feel. That is the difference meditation makes in your body and mind.

XVIII.
The Path

We are given our path as we enter the world.

Now, the sun has risen on the day. Every living thing begins to waken. The birds are singing a song of creation. The worms go underground and I hear the grass growing. The cycle of life is comforting. For as we are born, we grow and live. Then in the winter of our lives we go to our final resting place, only to join the others in the heavens.

How will it be to feel that peace, to finally leave this weary body? On a day such as this I scarcely imagine leaving, yet it is coming soon. It is my motivation now. To ensure that the movement will flourish and to arrive at my final resting place. As I move forward in my day, I ask for the divine support of those who have gone before me. I feel their love and know I can do what I must.

That is to sew my broken heart one stitch at a time, for it has been torn apart by life's events.

There are a thousand stitches in my heart holding it together from this earthly experience. I am weary of soul. At times I wonder how I'll make it to the next chapter of my life.

Knowing, changing and hoping for a peaceful end, I travel on. I wish to make demands of this time in my journey. Is it too much to ask to stay in one place for the rest of my days?

Cannot those truth seekers come to me? That is my demand. I can no longer travel as I once did and the day is long.

Holding onto my cherished memories, as I sit dozing by a fire.

Yes, that is my wish Dear Ones, to retire. I make it so by the will of my soul. No matter the wishes of others. No matter the path, I am done now. Never saying no, and though willing to sacrifice to spread the word I have complied to do so. Of one thing I did agree as I knew my life would be one of sacrifice. Service and serving can be done in many ways. I pledge to finish my part from a home, at the end of my days. I have been alone all these years.

The night is upon us as the owl calls. We pray as we have done through time immemorial, thanking the Holy Ones, as our spirits endure. The fog descends as we bid good night.

XIX.
The Ah Ha Moment–
Evolution and the Divine Path.

The truth takes us down many roads and the choice to speak it is ours. The choice of truth presents consequences, but we always have a choice, Dear Reader.

Your choices are yours to make, no one else. When negative consequences follow from a choice you have made, do not blame another. Accept that consequences occur and make the best of it. I hear you saying, "but what about the poverty stricken, the sick and maimed, surely they did not choose that path?" All we know at present is the path they have before them and they must walk it. We can only stay true to our own path and be sure not to judge another's path. If you can help those less fortunate that yourself, then do so.

Have we made our peace? What that means

can be subjective. What is peace to you? Do you ever feel peace? It can be as simple as a feeling of being HOME.

Dear Reader, when you travel somewhere new, upon your arrival a first impression of feeling warmth and familiarity— that is peace; that is a sense of home. How wonderful to discover this portal from the past that allows you to breathe and feel more alive! Now heartfelt and grateful you are filled with a sense of wonder.

How can this be you muse... that I am able to discover new beginnings at my age? It is your birthright and it is waiting for you, as it has been throughout the centuries.

When you feel an inkling of a connection wherever that may be, and wonder why... follow the feeling. It is a thread which leads to a part of yourself that is unknown. Pay attention to details that fill you with awe and wonder. These are a roadmap to a yet undiscovered sense of self that will surprise you. This is leading you to an awareness of your soul at the deepest level.

In following the thread, we are also sewing the thread Dear Reader. For we all fit together in the fabric as it is sewn. Like puzzle pieces we fit together and cannot exist one without the other.

Sometimes people lead us to the thread as if they are a needle, guiding, straight and sharp through the other threads of the fabric. For each of us has a singular purpose. Discovering it brings peace for some. For others, the thought of changing everything in their life may cause distress.

In the instance of unfulfilled purpose, we can be unhappy and impatient to move forward. But as long as you are aware of your gift and can help others in your daily life, it will come to fruition in its time. *For every single step one takes on the path leads to a moment of self-discovery.*

As we discussed, it can take a lifetime, sometimes less or more. But rest assured that if you follow your heart and radiate happiness and goodwill toward others in a helpful way, the Universe will provide for the unveiling at the right moment. The exact moment that resonates with your soul is the right moment. At that instance one's life changes forever. Be also aware that *readiness to change leads to the point of no return for the "old self."*

Do not fear! One does not engage in the journey until one is ready. The wonder and emotion when the realization sets in is a part of the process. It is meant to be, for at times one may feel overwhelmed by the amazing transformation. Like the caterpillar in the chrysalis, evolving and growing until the moment its shiny, colorful wings have developed to allow it to fly. Are you ready to fly?

XX.
Sunrise Sacrifice

With the Sunrise comes the pure sacrifice of the One.

As I ride to meet the Sun, the morning dew is heavy on my cape. I know not whether I will return from where I go. To recognize my fear while in the deep knowledge of my path is a choice I make each day. Throughout the ages we light bearers follow a path of choices.

It is set forth before us when we are born, like a written song... we follow the notes which complete the melody. What song will you sing? Which music is your life playing, Dear One?

To be able to hear the song is a gift we have inside of us. We must listen in the silence to hear our unique music. It is our path to follow, but given and chosen in agreement with the Collective Consciousness. You may say it is

God or the Creator or Source. We all make up the Consciousness of the planet, that is our total connection to each other. We are all a thread in the fabric of the world and without each thread the fabric has no strength. Your song, that no other human hears, is the path shown to you, so that following your heart is the answer.

I feel a lightness of being, a fullness of love that is indescribable with the knowledge that I go in love on the path chosen by the One. I can bear witness to all things!

I am unafraid as I travel to the unknown; alive with the feeling of victory in conquering my fear. Each of us must go into the world facing our fears and doubts, for we all experience them at some point. Every person throughout time has doubted whether they were making the right choice. Although knowing in their heart and led by faith, they carried onward.

$XXI.$
Walking the Path

In many ways, the fact that you are reading these words reveals where you are on the path. You are ready and Universe is supporting you. It is there for you to discover! Just waiting like a door to be opened. You are alive in the moment and you are loved. Go ahead... open the door.

What will you do with your gift? Now that you have it in your hand and keep it in your heart, the road may become more difficult. Be calm, be still, know that you are loved. Prayer and meditation each day helps to reunite you with the source. Center and focus come through daily practice and your strength builds until it becomes a natural state for you. You will want to discipline yourself to meditate daily because it leads to peace.

How are we to handle these difficulties or negativity in our daily lives?

"From the dark we can only see the light."

Think of this concept for a moment. In the dark you cannot see except for the light that shines.

When you feel yourself in a difficult situation or feel impending negativity, try to bring forth positive feelings that bring joy. Try to figure out where the negative feeling comes from and then you can work to dispel it. If it comes from fear, realize what it is that you are afraid of losing, such as control, money, job or your status.

Do not be afraid. You can overcome anything. When circumstances change in life, we are recreating all the time with our thoughts. Think of what you love doing. Then see yourself doing it, each day in a happy way. Feel it, smell it, hear it. Believe in the magic of your creation. You will soon see it come to fruition.

XXII.
Sing Love

The morning dew on the grass fills me with wonder at the simple miracles of life. The dew feeds the grass and the tiny insets and the growth of it all feeds the birds; on ward flows the circle of life. Through this same pattern we follow a cycle of life, growth, death and rebirth of the soul.

The soul lives on and transgressing the planes of existence known to those who have gone before us, carries us through the transition between death of the body and the new life we will live in spirit. These experiences are not known to us as human beings inhabiting a body. We can access this level of existence through meditation or other forms of soul travel, like a near death experience for example. Mainly we want you to have no fear and to believe in the goodness of the Collective

Consciousness, which we help to develop through kindness, spiritual belief and prayer.

There is only love. Though some in your world choose to act out of hatred and fear, it does not define humanity; it only raises you up to do more good and to combat fear with love.

For if all of you believe it and create it, the reality will occur at once. Yes, it takes work and coming together as one mind with a purpose to create a new world. One world where everyone is equal, where there is no difference between races and all men, women and children are one. In thought, that ideal can be accomplished now.

How so, you may ask. By focusing on the pure feeling of love and service to others. Love your fellow human, trust in the Universe to provide for your needs and go out into the world and do good works. Make helping others your aim in all you do, whatever your profession or motivation. Be guided by inspiration to help others.

XXIII.

Your Place in the World.

Awareness requires an alertness to the possibilities surrounding us. Having addressed the tenets of awareness in each part of your life, we now focus on the larger picture: your place in the world as an awakened soul.

Be alive! Be awake! What can you do today to further love in the world? It may be simple, like helping an elderly person with a heavy load. Or it can be more complex. Apply your gift how and when you are able. It is as plain as that, for once you discover your gift you cannot hold it back. Share it and use it to help, to encourage, to be an example to others through your kindness and light.

As you remember the lives and memories of a life before, try and bring the best parts forward into who you are now. All the while, give thanks and be grateful for the moment in time that is NOW.

Amongst human relationships, yes, there is love. The type of love I speak of is beyond human love; it is all the love of the Collective Consciousness speaking to us and trying to get our attention. For where is this kind of love when we need it the most? If we focus on the material and build our lives upon it we may never know this mystery and magic. It is that to be sure, it is magic!

When you stand in your power, aware that you can create anything and help others do the same, it is a powerful, positive feeling.

And finally, upon realization, the common refrain is "wow, it's so simple. I would have done it already if I knew how simple it is." Therein lies the difficulty for humans, we do not believe that having it all as a divine unit of God, is a simple act of faith. We believe it must be a lifelong hardship to accomplish based on our conditioning. You are God, you come from the Creator and the Collective Consciousness of this world and beyond. Accept your birthright. Discover your gift and become aware. Your life depends on it.

Those who hear truth will hear yours and you theirs. Be not afraid of disrobing in front of the world to reveal the real you. Your life holds many wonders just waiting there for you to allow it. You are meant for this moment in time.

Trust in faith and the inner sense of who you truly are and all will be well. And so it shall be, for the gift you carry is a gem sparkling with the treasure of your soul, shining for all to see. It is time to share your gift.

$\mathcal{XXIV}$.
A Vision of Flying

Adream occurs to me as I have a vision of flying in the desert.

As I walk upon the dusty road it rises up to envelop me, the heat a stasis for my soul. I travel down a path few choose. As I gaze at the golden desert, vivid images rise before me like a mirage. They waver, shine and pull me into the dream. I float willingly, swimming into the scene. I feel a lightness and have no physical form at all. I fly everywhere at once and I leave behind my dusty existence to glide away into freedom. Freedom of my soul exists in this realm; it is glorious! The world vanishes below, as I witness true wonders in my mind's eye, for as a spirit I have no eyes to see with. Surrounded by feeling, by spirit, by love, I explode with the ecstasy of this moment in eternity.

Soaring, I'm blissfully aware of all the other souls along for the ride! Onward we go as far as we can to experience a timeless, weightless center of being, showing us what we will see when we leave our bodies and transition to the other side of existence. What a joyous time to join with my soul group and confirm what I've felt through many lifetimes. That we are ether and one day reunited with all those we love and cherish. I fall back from the heights of vision, no longer flying. Transcending the veil, I go back to my body on this dry, dusty road in the golden desert I so love. No longer, flying but bolstered by my vision and traveling on the journey with renewed hope and love, to share, to inspire and serve another day.

XXV.
Let Your Light Shine

Your light is like the sun; seeking... sleepy in the morning and slowly rising to meet the day and light the way for all to see. Let it shine! As it travels the sky through its different phases it has various meanings for us. It shines brighter at noon and starts setting at dusk.

What will you do with your light? Will you keep it hidden from others for fear of being labeled "different?" the self-realization haunting you, while your gift is stowed away?

Dear Reader, I kept my light from others. I was afraid to be different. Slowly, but surely, I became aware and self-actualized. As I was seeking, I met my spiritual family and started making immense changes in my life. If I was still hiding my light at least I was on the path toward freedom.

Zero in on your fear. Is it a loss of income, status

or acceptance that causes the fear of revealing your true self? It is so, all of this may occur, but living in darkness is not truly living. And living in the material world limits the beauty and love that is available to you.

You may reason that you have a nice car, a nice home, or nice clothes. Well, Dear One, can you really derive so much pleasure from a car? Do you feel completely at peace and fulfilled? I'm not so sure, do you feel that something is missing?

As we have reviewed, if you practice meditation and focus on the inner self then questions arise from the depth of who you truly are at the soul level.

Many people have achieved wealth and fame and are perceived to "have it all", yet they still seek truth and a fulfillment for that empty feeling inside.

That missing piece is the awareness of belonging to the greater fabric that is the patchwork quilt of life, combining all other threads. Your gift is the thread that weaves within the others, to bring it all together recognizing the connection.

Again, review your life to find the meaning there, and what makes your soul sing.

Are you able to go into the world each day with a happy heart, knowing that circumstances cannot alter your joy? Because it is true, nothing can change who you were born to be at the soul level. Nothing can change your unique gift. But it is up to you to share it with the world and help make the world a better place.

$XXVI.$
Calling on Faith

"To live the faith, to feel the faith and to bring the faith to all who hear the call."

That message was the true essence of our calling in the early days. Having nothing BUT faith and true brotherhood through friendship made that calling an easy one to assume. The beauty of all around us was intoxicating. We felt we could accomplish anything with the support surrounding us as we were exiled, yet fully awake in moving forward the One Love with the Word of God. Our faith sustained us. Our friendships supported us. Our love protected us.

As we go, there we are, as our mantra points out truthfully. We were on the path of something much larger than ourselves. To continue delivering the word as brought to us by the One. Confident, present and with love, we knew our purpose. We loved this holy place as our first sanctuary after exile from the homeland, and would return to it over and over throughout our lives, for hundreds and thousands of years. In other incarnations of course, that is. Glastonbury, a beacon of light; it led us out into the world and beyond. And as a beacon, it welcomed us back from our travels. From near and far we have the bearings lodged in our inner compass forever. Always welcome, as a mother who wraps her arms around you with unconditional love no matter the circumstances. We love, we fear and we die. We return in the form of our choosing to live again and again, bringing our faith.

When we have lost our way, it feels as though we may never be happy or feel safe again. But in the dark, there is always light, like a candle glowing. Follow the light to your purpose and you will be forever on the path of devotion. **Calling on our faith, we sustain our souls by the very purpose we seek.** Though we know not what it is it sustains like a mantra or a prayer. We use it in times of need, a feeling of purpose that is there inside of you.

$XXVII.$
Receiving Unconditional Love

To experience unconditional love one must be ready, for receiving it is as important as giving it. When a child offers its parent unconditional love in the form of a smile, an embrace or a kiss, it must be received, accepted and returned. That is how the unbreakable bond is created. The same type of love occurs between siblings, extended family, lovers and friends. Accept what you are to receive and see the good in all.

Don't let self-loathing or self judgement keep you from having love in your life. Your children need you in a non-judgmental way. Be kind to them and be present in their company. And do the same throughout your daily activities; experience the here and now to allow for synchronicity to flow in your life.

Look at all the world's leaders in faith, science, thought, etc... Gandhi, Saint Joan of Arc, Jesus of Nazareth, Saint Mother Teresa, Albert Einstein, the originators of the United States of America Bill of Rights, Benjamin Franklin, Martin Luther King, Jr. All of these individuals followed a single-minded path even knowing that they may die for having done so. For them, it was not enough to live in fear; they led the way on the path of truth and light in order to hear their song. Many did die in their fight for freedom or truth. And without their courage, our world would be a different place as we know of the gifts they brought to bear in terms of enlightenment, inventions, individual freedom and much more.

The main point is clear. Follow your heart, listen to your individual song and face your fears and doubts in order to become more fully alive! You will feel ecstasy like no other, knowing that you are the only one who can hear your song and play your tune. That is your gift. Share it with all and weave the fabric tighter and stronger until, as a whole fabric, we eventually have no more tears or holes in it. As a unified force we can accomplish anything.

We ask the Collective Consciousness to help us on the path and provide what is required to follow our calling in faith and love. That is why we are all here on the planet now.

XXVIII.
The Way

And with our light, the way was made clear... we carried the message of unconditional love on our journey. Riding and walking to wherever God led us to do the work. As we individually went our separate ways, we each made our own movement, in a sense. We called on others to join us and deliver the word, to carry on once we were gone. We expanded the circle until we grew old and settled in one place. And even then, we continued to deliver God's word in our homes and where we lived. Our love for one another, our bond, would never be broken. Nor could it be broken. Oh, how I long for those days now, as I grow old and many have long since departed. I long for the unbreakable bond sewn with love, Love of God, love of each other and our families. The comfort of being part of such an instrumental tool of the faith movement is a feeling one is not able to describe in words.

I carry it in my heart each day and pray that I can continue to bring the light into the world. The purpose of sharing this love is to raise up the planet and change the dynamic back to love as its currency. To sew the threads within the fabric of life, to make it strong and enduring.

For this Dear Ones, is the real mystery of life. Nothing more. To love and be loved. To care for each together with genuine feeling, building the vibration that carries us forth on the path of truth. Seekers, all of us, carrying the lantern in the dark, sometimes not knowing that which we seek but propelled by an unseen force, one that cannot be ignored. For the effort is the key to our survival. And without we will perish. LOVE not fear, peace not war; calm not chaos that is the way. Our bodies and our earthly things may remain in the dark, but the soul of light and love does not. These all die or leave, and the way forward is shrouded in darkness and fear. Your voice, your truth, your love, yes, it is there and alive! Use it on the true path of enlightenment to bring the world together as one. We are all one; we are all the same. As it was in the beginning and ever shall be.

We must stay true to the cause and continue the fight. You who feel the drive, know who you are, the drive to deliver the truth and light the way no matter the cost. Delve into your heart, unlock the secret door to your gift and tell us the tale. So many are waiting and need to hear the ways to true happiness. It is there for you, just turn the key. Join the truth seekers and lead the way. Trust, love, truth and light let those virtues be your guide.

XXIX.
Our Gift

Go forth in your faith, in your purpose, and light the way for others in the dark. And that Dear Reader is our gift. The gift we were born with and will die with, unique in its make-up, for without it why would be here at all?

Be hopeful and helpful. Be happy and present. Rely on faith in difficult times, and maintain hope that you will get through it. Hold tight to the idea that your journey bears a purpose, and to the faith that *the struggles, as they appear, will not last forever.*

Change your perspective and you change the energy of the situation. *Focus on what you want in life!* Try not focusing on the negative. Be the change you wish to see in the world—light the way with your unique purpose and each day will be brighter! The Universe has a plan for each of us; allow the plan to coalesce while doing your best each day to move forward.

To say there is no hope can never be true. There is always hope in any life lesson.

How do I know this you ask? Because the mere act of believing is the energy of change. I can tell you that I have seen this in my own life. Believing in hope can create new possibilities!

There may be times in your life that you are in despair and feel that your life will never be the same. And it may not, yet it will hold magic, faith and happiness again if you allow the feelings into your consciousness.

I have been in that situation, I do know the feeling of despair in this life and others. I have been in deep despair, but I prevailed.

I did so with the support of family and friends but mainly I did so by relying on my deep faith in the Source of all things to provide for me, and I allowed the workings of the Universe to take over while I did my best to move forward daily. I practiced positive thinking, mindfulness and a drive to find happiness again.

I also knew and know that I had a destiny to fulfill and that I was not finished living yet.

Know that life changes daily, Dear Reader, just swim in the tide flowing, now against it. Eventually you will get to where you want to be and where you need to be. Be grateful for all that you DO have instead of what you feel you don't have. Be happy, it is a new day, make the most of it!

XXX.
Parting

The Sun rose without fanfare, the sky a pale blue. Clouds fluffed and drifted slowly past my vision, a scent in the air of wet grass and earthy vegetation. As I gaze upon the sea that surrounds me, my soul is grateful for all that has blessed our existence here. Sacred ground, friends and followers, peaceful days and dream filled nights have eased the pain of loss.

The memories of our One Lord and the horror of his demise will never leave us, yet we know the reasons for the event in this life. They haunt us forever, yet we chose this path long ago.

To know the mission is complete imbues me with a sense of finality. To be given this respite is a blessing and my heart will forever be filled with gratitude and deep love for our time here.

In many ways, I do not wish to go forward

into the future. Sometimes I feel that prayer and serenity are my favored destiny. As my eyes take in the simple, natural beauty of the landscape I say a prayer for all who dwell here to remain in peace forever. The heart energy of The Tor is here forever and will hold a piece of my heart.

I feel with sadness it is my time to leave here. I am ready to go to my final resting place as it has been foretold, and remain there until my death. I shall live out my old age in solitude, writing the word of the One Lord, as I know it. Never straying far from my path as keeper of the word, which is my role in so many ways. I again follow the steps down from the Tor, climbing down to a reality that awaits me.

The sojourn has come to an end. Parting ways with my brothers and sisters is bittersweet and we must carry on the movement. In some ways relieved, I rest my weary soul. I feel it is my time to be at peace and write the story of the One True Love.

My heart is full as the others continue on their course. I stay behind and bid farewell to my dearest companions. So much is behind us now. Although we risk persecution, we know of others in our group who are here and beyond. We all go in our different directions, a bond of love forever between us.

$\mathcal{XXXI}$.
Daily Practice

F irst, it's imperative that you take time to be STILL... away from distraction, noise, people. Then, listen to your heart. Does your heart sing? Or is it crying? What does your heart need to be nourished?

This is a key to learning about yourself. *For your heart is the key to your soul. Learn the secret in your heart and you learn to live the heart soul connection.* Then, and only then are you truly following your path. The lantern you hold in your heart shines on the path that leads to happiness.

The quiet place in your soul has a story to tell and that story is your gift. The gift you bring to the celebration of life is one no other can share. For we each have our own way to help others rise to the full height of their soul purpose.

The earth's purpose is the collective mission

of all who inhabit it. In order to participate, we must be on the path to knowing ours and helping others learn what their path is, so we can together change the planet.

And so, Dear Reader that is our mission. Weave your thread through the fabric, make it strong so that we are all joined as one. In the fabric of life, each thread matters. We are all connected to the whole.

Love or fear; those are the options for responding to life as we know it. If you choose fear, you will feel worse. If you choose love, you will share it and you will feel happy by doing so with the reward of unselfish focus.

Know yourself first—as we discussed in the beginning of our time together. How do you try to become aware of who you are? What is your perception of your soul and how it relates to the Collective Consciousness or the rest of the souls you inhabit your daily life with throughout your life?

In the quiet of the moment when you feel the stillness of your soul... listen.

XXXII.
Farewell

Retire to my abode of little occasion, to begin my days that take me to the end of this life. I now serve as watch woman for the sacred word. Those who follow our movement may come on a journey here and I will show the way. That is my path now, Guide of the Seeker, providing respite for the weary; Light in the Dark. As swept up as I am by the emotion of a farewell, I am content to know I will stay in one place now. Tis comforting by the fire to sit and rest and write.

As I doze once more into dreaming, I see the memories of my life. Such sweet love we had all of us together, so innocent and pure. We felt each day that nothing could touch this perfection. Simple, yet true. Then the world changed as foretold. Knowing and then feeling it happen are not quite the same.

The pain subsides, yet a hole remains where the living joy of my True Love once was, now with me in spirit. I feel his loss each day. With all I know and though I am a woman of faith, I still feel it; time does not erase the deepest wounds. I allow my human feelings to rise up to the surface of this moment, keenly felt. Many memories are flowing through me, as a movie in front of my eyes.

I know I'll see him soon as I prepare to leave my body now. My life's work here has been an effort to make it through, at times, insurmountable odds. Yet, perpetual love and faith has enabled me to follow the path I was given and accepted as my destiny. The knowing is what keeps me sane. I know I'm meeting my loved ones in spirit of which we originated, surrounded by love— a love unknown in this realm of life. I long for the time to arrive, yet say farewell to my life here on earth. Tis a strange image which presents itself in front of me. I am able to see the journey of my life here as well as the one that awaits me. I sigh with relief. I know the time is near as I am surrounded by my Angels and my loved ones. My heart is full to bursting with purest love. I rest and wait for the end of my days. I am at peace. I trust that I am in alignment with my divine right. The silent sentinel awaits by the door. I rise up, a light... no longer a body. I fly away with my loved ones and the Angels. I float through their wings as light as air! I go now.

XXXIII.
Conclusion

The wind caresses me as I gaze into the present moment. Echoes of voices from long ago haunt me in this energy. The children are ever present in spirit. Have we brought them in this incarnation? Who are they? Tumbling, laughing and crying... the presence of childlike energy keeps us sane.

Coronations, weddings, birth and death. The cycle the Ancients foretold provides us with the wisdom to continue on.

The cold wind is a reminder of what lies ahead. Winter brings endings and spring brings new beginnings. Just like the child, ever present, ever timeless. The flowers bloom, grow and fade, as do our lives. Each one unique, each one much the same. We mourn for a long-ago way of life that equals a perfect humanity to us. Memories and feelings ebb and flow. We want the past yet move forward into the present and its future. We do so in acceptance of all that is, as it is, in respect for the web of life.

The bird calls bring me back to the present moment. Reflection is gone now, along with wind... blowing us forward, ever present!

The jewels of our memories twinkle and their light remains forever. Carry them in your heart for future hardships. Open the jewel box to receive the vibration of love. Strive for openness and humanity to bring together those in need. For that is a gift you bring to the celebration of life.

Author's Note: It is a choice, this path we take, to bring the word to those who hear and seek the truth. It is a commitment and lifestyle like no other. At times we are beaten down for our beliefs and words. Sometimes it is like a dream, wonderful to be surrounded by the people of the light. The dream I remember is Glastonbury. My home of homes where my soul resides like the ancient graves within the Abbey ruins, I am also there in spirit. My love, my soul, is buried there.

Resurrected by the coming together of a special group in this lifetime, I feel such immense gratitude for this reunion of souls. It was like I reawakened at last to live in peace and light. With the experience emblazoned upon my heart forever, I remain thankful.

Epilogue

It has not been without a lot of disruption, distraction, trial and tribulation and sadly, death— that I have composed and published this book. It is also with much inspiration, support and belief in my work from my soul group, that I have been able to complete it. It is a message from Source, as channeled through me, for those who seek and wish to know themselves.

I have also written a work-book to accompany this material, called "Putting Awareness Into Practice." The exercises will assist you on a daily basis to actually do the work of becoming aware. It will be available soon!

ORIGINS

As I was attending a Conscious Writing retreat in Glastonbury, Somerset, UK, in May of 2015, I was inspired to channel and write this material. Well, now it is January of 2018.

I knew upon becoming aligned with my creative consciousness, through Conscious Writing, that I would then have to integrate a new awareness into my daily life. This led to many changes. Business relationships, personal relationships all changed in various ways. My outlook changed completely with regard to business which led to working with different sectors as I felt more inclined to work with organizations who were helping others.

While I had written the book in longhand, I then typed and edited and finally had the manuscript edited by a soulful, steadfast editor, Nivi Nagiel. My thanks to her for sticking by me and honoring the spirit of the message.

My marriage was then struggling due to financial considerations. At the time, my husband fully supported me in writing the book, but he eventually decided to focus on his business. During the two years I was writing and editing my book, I wholeheartedly supported his endeavors through my marketing expertise and now he has a very successful business, which opened in December of 2015. We then we ended our marriage in Summer of 2017.

I succeeded due to the support from family

and friends, and especially— my Mom to whom I am eternally grateful. All the while, I was part of a dedicated and loving team of my son Anthony, family and friends as we cared for my other mother, Barbara. She was dying and we provided support and love to her in those final days. She never lost her sense of humor or her grace during the last five months of her life. She passed away in November of 2017. She is always with me by my side and is a source of inspiration as she fully supported me in this book, and understood its significance.

So, while it seems like time has passed and delayed the publishing of this material, it has not been without its intended lessons and life experiences which all played a large part in my ability to be genuine in this endeavor. All in divine timing as they say! And, I would not really clearly know the meaning of self-care without having gone through this episode in my life, and I would not be able to really speak to it with clarity. For it was in the afore mentioned instances that I did rise up and finally learn to put myself first in various ways as a mother, as a wife, as a person, and finish my book and get it published.

I do so wish that this message helps you realize a dream, provides hope or a new focus towards your highest good. Its aim is to assist you in discovering your true gift to help others and raise the vibration of our planet.

About the Author

S usan began exploring self awareness in the early 80's as a result of reading Brian Weiss, MD's book, "Many Lives Many Masters," and attending his workshops. After moving to Atlanta as a member of the Georgia Lottery start-up team, her self-actualization quest included studying many spiritual practices, a favorite guru being Self Realization Fellowship Founder, Paramahansa Yogananda. A veteran public relations and internet marketing professional over a highly substantive 30 year career, Susan traveled around the world seeking answers and received them in the form of the International Conscious and Creative Writing Association and founder Julia McCutchen. This led to attending a retreat in Glastonbury, UK in May of 2015, where the words of this book flowed forth in a torrent of inspiration. Becoming aligned with a creative consciousness provided the impetus to write and complete this book, and begin a poetry blog which is accompanied by her Florida nature photography.

Susan resides in West Palm Beach, Florida and Atlanta, Georgia, where she works, writes, reads and take photos of nature. To find out more visit: http://snefzgerpr.wordpress.com.

35264609R00073

Made in the USA
San Bernardino, CA
08 May 2019